Being a series of essays disclosing the **SOCK MENACE** that threatens our world.

By
MADAME HORROR and DOODLEMONKIE

- A SOCK HORROR PUBLICATION -

© 2007 Charlotte Yates & Ian Terry. All rights reserved.

The rights of Charlotte Yates and Ian Terry to be identified as the authors of this work have been asserted to them in accordance with the Copyright, Designs and Patents Act, 1988.

This book is sold subject to the condition that it shall not, by way of trade or otherwise be lent, resold, hired out, or otherwise circulated without the publisher's prior consent in any form of binding or cover other than that in which it is published and without a similar condition, being imposed on the subsequent purchaser.

ISBN-13 978-0-9556922-0-8

Acknowledgements
MH: Thanks to Rob for putting up with my 'creative strops' and being so supportive. Thanks also to my parents for embracing the thought processes that helped create this and providing encouragement throughout.
And also to DM for seeing the potential.
To Rachel and Paul, my official humour gauges.

DM: Thanks to Diane, Lewis and Rebecca, for your continued faith and support. Also thanks to VA Terry, for proofing and suggestions.
To MH for her unique concept, without which this book would not exist. Thank you for allowing me into your strange and wonderful world!
Thanks to Tom for hooking monkies up with horrors.

SOCKMOSIS

What is Sockmosis?

For centuries, mankind has pondered the nature of the universe, looking up to those heavens at night, considering worlds that may lie beyond theirs. In more recent times, some have even wondered what threats may lurk out there, in the inky nothingness of space, writing stories of impossible intelligences that see Earth as a resource for their greedy needs, invading in saucers and wreaking havoc on all fronts.

But what if it were possible? That a force – completely alien to us – were to intrude upon our world when we least expect it? What if it were not only possible, but going on right now, perhaps in your very home? Would you be ready? Where would you expect this danger to come from? Who would be so bold?

Consider this. Perhaps it is an enemy not from the skies above us, but from what lies beneath our very feet. For the lowliest place has spawned the most unlikely foe of all…

Welcome to **Sockmosis.** You have in your hands one of the parts of a series of essays, observations and writings, generated through extensive research and investigation, that will give you all you need to know; a series of books that in time may come to be your survival manual. Because what you learn here will change the way you see the world, and after that, things will never be the same again.

We Are Under Attack (From Under)

Two things need to be understood. Neither of them is easy to hear, let alone comprehend. Brace yourself; if you are not seated, you may wish to do so.

1. It is going on right now and It cannot be stopped.

That's right. We are in it for the long haul. There is no easy fix or magic solution. But it isn't too late to know about this new terror – which brings us to the second part: the enemy.

2. Your Socks are your Enemy. You can no longer trust your socks.

You probably have trouble grasping the concept that laundry can be anything at all, other than laundry. You might even think it a rather eccentric idea – outlandish, even. Perhaps even completely insane. That's ok, we get that a lot. It takes time.

To those people we simply say this. Read this volume, perhaps investigate our other publications. Give the matter some thought. We guarantee that you will never look at your socks in quite the same way again – especially when the ones you own – the ones you think you know - go missing.

'Madame Horror has carved her bloody way into the world'

Sockmosis serves to demonstrate the findings and observations of two of the worlds foremost authorities on this new threat.

Through the study and observation, dissection and preservation, Madame Horror has carved her bloody way into the world of the doldrites and has come back with more information than any respectable scientist thought possible.

Aided and abetted by her loyal companion, Professor Doodlemonkie, a reclusive fringe academic, noted for his vast knowledge of myth and lore, as well as a somewhat reputable crypto zoologist, Madame Horror is for the first time about to tell her story to an unsuspecting world.

It's quite a yarn.

NOTE: All observations are accurate at time of publication. Investigations are ongoing and conclusions are subject to change in light of new analysis. The information we present to you here has been collected by continued questioning of captured doldrites and extensive (sometimes dangerous) experimentation and should only be conducted by a trained professional.

Contents

Introduction..7
Foreword..9
The Doldrites Vs. The Human World..........11
Sockmosis 15
      Muster Missions...................................16
      Sockophiles and Sockophobes..................17
Into the Fray..19
      Radiator Veterans 21
      Distinction & Extinction 22
      Muddle Mischief 24
      Sleeper Depravation 25
Journey's End..27
Conclusion 29

Appendices

Map of The Doldrums...................................32
Region Spotlight: The Midflats.......................33
The Garden of Mislaid Garments #1: the stocking eel....35
The Secret World of Sockmosis.........................39
Dust Bunny Snuff...42
Excerpts from the Book of Brutality..................43
Further Reading...51
Classifieds...55

Foreword

When Worlds Collide is the first of a series of books that form the **Sockmosis** investigations. It primarily focuses on the conflict between the hostile *doldrites* – inhabitants of a different universe to us – on the one side and we, the human race, on the other.

Here you will find out everything we have learned about the doldrites and what they seek in our world; their habits and rituals when they arrive here and the all-important selection process that forms their raid. You will discover how we believe they commute between their world and ours; how they specially select households - including yours - for their guerrilla missions, and to what perilous ends they must go in order to secure a route back home.

Understanding the enemy is perhaps the most important part in any war. This volume sets out to uncover the dark truths that shroud our lives. And feet.

The Doldrites vs. The Human World

For some time now (precisely how long is uncertain), our world has been repeatedly invaded by a previously unseen foe: not from the far reaches of the cosmos, but from a universe that exists in and around our lives; invisible to see, impossible to touch. Our presence in this world was as unknown to them as their world is to us.

But at some point, things changed. Somehow, they found a way to pass through from their reality to ours, with the specific intention of plundering our world – our own homes – of a resource much prized by these unwelcome visitors. Searching for a specific component, they perform lightning raids (usually by cover of night), locating and abducting their quarry without us even knowing, other than a strange sensation the next morning; a feeling of loss and forgetfulness…

This is what we know: these strange invaders are called *doldrites*. They come to us from a world (called *The Doldrums*) very different to ours, and are composed of different base material to us, with a diversity of type and design that has taken many laborious hours of study and classification (the report on this analysis can be found in *Sockmosis: Anatomy of a Doldrite*). These doldrites have a very specific method for what they do - through the course of this volume, we will be looking at their ways and means of thievery.

It appears that doldrites are not so much born as created, emerging from a bizarre primordial ooze after being dunked, in egg form, into this goop. The vessel that is used as an egg absorbs a highly complex chain of chemicals that very quickly produces spontaneous growth, resulting in a fully formed doldrite in minutes. All the ingredients for this miraculous life can be found in The Doldrums, with one major exception – the very vessel required for doldrite life: a sock.

That's right – in order to make a doldrite, their people must first immerse a sock into the ooze, and this must be a sock taken from the human world. Why this is, or came to be, is a source of great debate amongst the scholars of The Doldrums (and a question we have discussed no end) and many theories and theologies have grown from this premise. But it is believed that, at some point at the very start of the known universe, a big bang happened, and some socks – or the cosmic equivalent of – were flung from what should be our universe and cast into some other reality instead, forming the very first doldrites.

It's a long debate which is fully explored in *Sockmosis: Genesis*, and a tale that needs telling. But time and space here restricts how much we can divulge in one volume, so instead we will assume your compliance with this premise for now; if not, then at least suspend disbelief for the time being as we describe to you their methods and plans, and then ask – is this so unfamiliar? Are you sure you are not already the victim of these criminals?

Inexplicably, the doldrites have discovered a way of breaching the barrier between our worlds, if only for a short while. Utilising a method known to the doldrites as *sockmosis,* a portal is opened between universes and remains open long enough for a small band of doldrites to pass through. This is what they refer to as a *muster mission* – a passage into the human world, with the intent of stealing socks to take back to The Doldrums.

Almost always operating under the canopy of darkness, a muster mission will begin when a portal is opened during sockmosis, as the party shifts from their dimension into ours. Crucially, this needs to be as near to human sleeping habitat as possible, but the location of the portal opening into the human world is fixed (more on this later) – so it may be necessary for the party to journey some distance to find their quarry. Importantly, the doldrites must also leave by a portal (not necessarily the one through which they arrived, however).

There are many dangers to the doldrites in our world, and many ways for them to die horribly (the unearthing of already deceased doldrites has resulted in the majority of our discoveries). The prospect of capture or confinement looms over each and every doldrite in the raiding party, with those missing the portal back forced into exile until they arrive on a method to return. Worse still, the return journey is by no means safe, as sockmosis is far from a perfect science in itself; many doldrites vanish completely, or die miserable deaths, or even end up as *string theory*. The journey back The Doldrums is far more dangerous than the journey into the human world.

A successful muster mission is one that has resulted in the stealing of one or more socks – although the doldrites see this as emancipation; freeing their assumed brethren from the tyranny of mankind. Socks returned to The Doldrums are nursed like eggs and ceremonially dumped into the Great Ooze, where healers wait to nurse the newly emerging doldrites, who will form their place in *The Legion*.

Sockmosis

Our current hypothesis states that to travel between their world and ours, the doldrites create a state of sockmosis between the universes. Specially charged objects (usually, human keys) are held against specific points, which may be suspended in the air, at any height, or even on the surface of a solid object. By introducing the charged object, the contact point – invisible to the naked eye - begins to shimmer, absorbing the static energy generated by the forces in The Doldrums. Soon, sockmosis occurs, creating a vortex of seemingly drenched matter, through which the doldrite crosses.

This portal can remain from anything to a few seconds to a few minutes, but as it closes, it does so quickly; anything not quite through is compressed and unravelled between the two worlds in an instant. So, naturally, great care must be taken when travelling by these means!

Muster Missions

Intensive questioning reveals that the chief (and perhaps only) purpose for the doldrite raids on our world is the location and acquisition of socks, either worn or unworn.

A muster mission is called by the Eldest Socks in The Doldrums – chief elders who oversee the running of their world. This council sets missions based on known targets, and will concentrate efforts into specific areas of the human world. On each Muster Mission, one doldrite on the mission is appointed party leader. Usually, this doldrite is chosen from the party by an Eldest Sock; however, even on covert missions, the tradition stays so that one natural leader is appointed. Almost always, this will be the *seeker* - being the caste that locate and rescue *sleepers* (the name given to socks in human possession), they are the obvious choice. However, it is not uncommon for a *muddle* or even a *healer* to be appointed Depredator.

The Depredator is charged with finding sleepers - discarded or stashed in one place - and coordinate the mission. This doldrite needs to be a resourceful, quick thinker, as the other party members will take guidance and instruction from the Depredator. If you are lucky enough to catch the depredator you can almost guarantee the rest will follow. Without their leader they are like lambs to the slaughter.

In order to liberate socks from the human world, doldrites must mount a muster mission to find and bring back as many sleepers as they can find. However, there is a physical limit to when this can be done, and how many can realistically be brought back to The Doldrums. To further complicate matters, the Eldest Socks like to exert control over these operations, and choose when and where rescues are mounted, attempting to coordinate matters with a war-like mindset, employing greater strategies. Eldest socks do not willingly travel to our world, believing the fate of their kind lies solely within their ability to orchestrate effective muster missions. However, Madame Horror has had the opportunity to study one of these dodrites and found nothing to authenticate their claim. Their perception of superiority is just that - an apparent perception and nothing more.

There are doldrites who think differently to the Eldest Socks and usually these are seekers looking for adventure and glory. As the *key keeper* has the final say (being the caste controlling the opening of portals to the human world), most seekers will consult with him and discuss their plans in the hope of being allowed into the human world. Needless to say, key keepers are young at heart and love to hear the stories young adventurers come back with, so as long as he is confident they will all return, he will usually issue them with a key.

Sockophiles and Sockophobes

Before we delve into the finer points of muster missions, it must firstly be pointed out that just as we are studying doldrites, so they are studying us. Just as we classify the new species we encounter, so have they classified humans. Luckily, their awareness at the present time does not extend beyond their need to free all sock-kind, but they are evolving at an astounding rate and their aptitude to adapt to any given situation is surprising. We need to be careful not to ridicule the future threat they pose.

We have learnt that, in a very sweeping generalisation, the doldrites have classified us into two main groups; *sockophiles* and *sockophobes*. There is a very wide disparity between the two - and we would argue a very grey area in between - but we have come to understand the distinction as follows:

Sockophiles are humans considered to have a penchant for socks. They love them, collect them, and spend hours ironing them and arranging them by day, colour, pattern, or all of the above. It appears however that their love of the sock is strangely reciprocal, as the sleepers in a sockophile household are also devoted to their master. This almost certainly results in a sleeper taking on human attributes being viewed as 'different' among doldrites and given the name *icons* to describe their kind.

Sockophobes are the humans at the opposite end of the scale to sockophiles. These humans hate socks, treat them with scorn and mistreat them in all sorts of ways. Sleepers rescued from sockophobes have so many abuse flashbacks that there is little chance of them ever recovering and will almost inevitably turn out to be a *gore*. An unfortunite doldrite destined to live out its days in search of a way to end it all in The Great Sock Off.

We contend that very few humans would identify themselves as either at one end of the scale or the other, but this is what we are deemed to be in the eyes of the doldrites.

Into the Fray

Although all sleepers are potentially future doldrites, our data indicates that seekers (specialist doldrites, charged with the task of locating socks) are particular about which sleepers they chose to appropriate. Numerous factors dictate those sleepers that are selected, from trivialities of positioning in the home and overall condition, to prejudices on breed and ensuring supply. The greatest skill of a seeker is locating the most desirable sleepers and assessing the potential dangers in making the acquisition. They understand the habits of humans and know the best places to look with the richest crops and least possibility of being noticed.

There are many technicalities to the selection process: it may be the sleeper is too obvious to take, having been placed carefully by a sockophile in a perfectly laid out pairing, or strewn carelessly on the floor by a sockophobe who will note the lack of laundry scattered about the bedroom. It is not to their advantage to remove these sleepers – instead, they will opt to investigate the hiding places that a human never looks at properly or that are well populated; the crevices between the bedroom furniture, the laundry basket or the sock drawer.

And do not be fooled that their expeditions are only conducted in your homes: in truth, they may appear anywhere they might find sleepers - laundrettes, hotels (now who hasn't lost a sock after a stay in a hotel?), or the gym. They also have a game that they find particularly amusing, where they pull the sleepers off the feet of infants while adults aren't looking.

Sometimes, muddles will use a rescued sleeper as a makeshift sack (called a *sockasack*), in which to put the collected sleepers and other stolen items, such as keys or watches. This is of course a resourceful use of an otherwise unconscious sleeper – however, unbeknownst to the doldrites, this seemingly harmless practice may be part of why some sleepers end up curiously affected by the human world, taking on behaviours and mannerisms that label such doldrites as *Icons*. We are coming close to identifying the process by which these changes occur.

It is our intention that in doing so we will be able to manipulate the characters of the resurrected sleepers and begin to control their success from within, as it were.

Another technique they use (which we affectionately call a *sock bite*) ensures a safe supply of sleepers while simultaneously inflicting pain on humans. It is quite a clever concept, indicating a level of acumen we afford few species.

The basis of the strategy is to remove a section of the

elastic from the cuff of the sleeper. This is a simple, routine operation that causes no long term effect to the sleeper in question, and can be accomplished on location. The result of this straightforward act is that the sock then becomes uncomfortable for the wearer who experiences, on occasion, a severe restriction of blood flow, exhibited by an imprint left around the ankle of the bearer of the weave of the sock. Oblivious to the incongruous fact that those same socks were satisfactory to wear on previous occasions, they are placed in the bin where they can be retrieved by the muster mission party on their subsequent visit.

Although the thought of getting caught is at the forefront of their attention, the potential of being discovered is not their only consideration. Their choice of sleeper is also dependent on its condition, with new and unworn socks being the most prized of all, providing an almost certain guarantee of perfectly formed and flawless doldrites who perform their duties without the impediment of abuse flashbacks. It is rare however to find sleepers in near perfect condition. The horrors to which sleepers are subjected to at the feet of humans are too numerous to mention here but are all documented in the ever growing tome they call *The Book of Brutality*.

Radiator Veterans

With the aim of the missions to free sleepers from *the long sleep* there is a particular type of sleeper all doldrites have a special affection for, for their suffering is virtually impossible to understand and as a consequence stimulates a great deal of sympathy. It also breeds hatred of humans in its purest form.

Contrary to what you may perceive, socks don't favour

being in warm dry places; they prefer cool, damper climates. As a consequence, socks that have become wedged behind the radiator are suffering a fate worse than death. A sleeper released from the confines of such incarceration will be found in a mummified state, rigid as the fibre reinforcing cures over an indefinite period of captivity. (We currently have an experiment mid- process involving the thorough examination of sleepers subjected to various stages of elevated temperature conditioning and we are generating some very interesting statistics; it is still early in the experiment, so no results will be divulged yet, but the findings may prove to be surprising).

These sleepers are transported back to The Doldrums with a reverence befitting royalty, where extended measures are taken in the rinsing process to help restore elasticity. However Radiator Veterans, as they are commonly known, are never as agile as their brethren and often feel a great deal older than their years would suggest. There is one gain to this eventuality though, after an extended period trapped where humans do not venture radiator veterans develop an innate understanding of fluff and find themselves naturally drawn to the role of *fluff herder*, a much valued responsibility in The Doldrums and absolute necessity for the healing of their kind.

Distinction and extinction

As hinted at earlier, doldrites are not without their discriminations. There are socks among your collection that would not be selected purely for their appearance: by this we do not mean the overall condition of the sock, but branding that may appear on it. Sleepers bearing markings of logos and merchandising are so offensive to doldrites they believe them to be beyond help. The philosophy that such symbols can be emblazoned on vulnerable sleepers with such disregard draws analogies to cattle branding or inking of slaves; consequently, these sleepers are considered too wretched to be saved.

As a way of subverting this, a seeker (the only caste with the constitution to carry out such acts) will set about rendering such socks useless, working at the stitching (often inferior anyway), or even sometimes fashioning holes and tears into the sock so that when the human puts it on, it rips through. This deed has a two-fold purpose; to put the sleeper out of its misery and to initiate the need of a human to buy more socks and hence guarantee a fresh supply.

Muddle Mischief

So, we have established that these intruders have created a way of invading our homes. But how do you know they have been if the only evidence is the fact that you have an odd sock or two? What if they have been very cunning, which of course they can be, and have helped themselves to matching pairs of socks (which in all fairness is more probable as you are less likely to notice a whole pair go missing).

Well, there are several ways to know if you have been paid a visit by these treacherous beings; and just as with the very obvious accumulation of odd socks, you have probably put it down to forgetfulness or distraction on your part; and that is their genius plan.

There is a caste of doldrites which we call *muddles,* which specialise in creating *muddle mischief.* It has been determined that every muster mission has at least one muddle in the party. Their main objective is to disguise the success of the seekers - a task in which they take great pride and employ several tactics. The easiest method, and most extensively used, is the hiding of small objects around your home; that scrap of paper with your aunt's telephone number on, the remote control for the television or the scissors (although this is more likely to be because scissors have blades - generally feared by doldrites).

However there are several things that are considered priceless and if they come across such an item it is taken back to The Doldrums. Most essential to their crusade is the gathering of keys, any key, and to a lesser extent objects that humans put a lot of energy into. These are given to the Key keepers to manage. Most of the time a bunch of keys is a prize too great to behold but it is a

hazard in itself. The nature and ability of keys to open portals is also their danger. A single additional key, brought through a portal can be controlled, but we can now confirm that several keys can be unpredictable with the possibilities of 'sidewinders' shooting off the true vortex and dragging a doldrite to an unknown location being a genuine risk. For that reason only small sets or single keys are taken.

Quite often, doldrites on a muster mission will chance upon a human's insole from a shoe. This was a concept that initially seemed to be without reason, and only recently has been found to have a purpose. These are always collected as an unexpected bonus by the accompanying muddle, to be added to the ever-growing collection of stolen insoles back in The Doldrums. Stolen insoles are made into party crowns and used as bunting for *Defunking Days*; however, the freshest of the crop (which is to say, the least used, and therefore richest in charcoals and other ingredients) are put aside for the annual *Insole Man Festival* during which the doldrites busy themselves for the duration of the downpour with the construction of a huge *Insole Man*.

Sleeper Depravation

The muster mission begins once the party arrives in the human world. Right from the alighting from the portal, the travelling doldrites get to work. The depredator will appoint the seeker the task of hunting out dormant socks; simultaneously, the accompanying muddle will set to work creating muddle mischief.

The main objectives of course are those socks, called sleepers by the doldrites. Sleepers are, for want of a better description, asleep; they have no knowledge, they have no desires, and they have no life. They are captive and are oblivious to it. Only once awoken in the land of The Doldrums do they find how they have been sedated and abused by their human captors.

The period of a sock's life in the human world has been termed *the long sleep*, where it lies dormant, waiting to be rescued, stuck in the world of the humans. The long sleep is over when a sleeper becomes a doldrite, back in The Doldrums, in a process they call *The Rinsing*. For some sleepers, this will never happen and the doldrite community hold vigils for such unfortunates that are destined for a life of slavery under the heel – literally – of their human masters.

Journey's End

We can be glad that once the travellers have found their quarry, they must return to a portal in order to make the perilous journey back home to The Doldrums and hope that they become victims of their own temperamental portal travel.

Assuming this portal is accessed without a hitch, the doldrites will ultimately find themselves back in their own world, where they can conclude their muster mission. The priority at this point will be to locate an eldest sock, who will scrutinise the prizes brought back into The Doldrums. This elder will attach instructions, called *footnotes,* for the sleepers (usually slipping a scrap of paper inside the sock), then commanding a party member to take the sleepers to a nearby *sock stack*, where in time they will then be dispatched to the healers on the banks of the rinising river to begin their transformation into doldrites.

These footnotes give any special orders to the healers, who will add special ingridients (if required) to the rinsing process, thereby influencing the outcome of the doldrite birth. By implimenting these instructions, a healer may be able to assure the production of certain doldrite castes. We have acquired one such footnote but as yet the scrawlings are not understood.

While the priority for the party is to deliver the sleepers to the eldest sock, it cannot be forgotten that the key used on the mission needs to also be returned to it's owner. This key keeper may be some distance from where the party are when back in The Doldrums, and it will often be the task of the most inexperienced, youngest or smallest doldrite to make the journey (sometimes taking many days) to the relevant keeper; many terrible tales are told to this poor doldrite as to what will happen if the key does not reach its destination, and suffice to say, it is claimed that no key has ever been lost.

Eventually, the sleepers will be transported in their sock stack to the rinsing river, and the happy task of bringing new life into The Doldrums begins. As the fresh doldrites emerge from the ooze, assisting healers begin to sort and classify them, by faction and by caste (none of these things will be certain, unless the footnotes enclosed in a sleeper dictate this). A simple enclosure acts as creche for the first couple of days, after which time each doldrite is assigned a home on one of the many archipelagos that spin endlessly in the microverse that makes up The Doldrums.

Conclusion

Do not feel sorry for these creatures. Yes, they face dangers in coming here, but can you really, in all honesty, condone the acts of malice they perform?

Much has been found out about the doldrites and their diabolical desires and has been recorded as discovered by Madame Horror and her companions. What has been covered in this tome merely scratches the surface of this complex conspiracy - but rest assured, we intend to document all we know. Look out for future publications, a list of which you will find at the end of this book (content summaries are included).

www.sockhorror.com

Maps & Appendices

Map of The Doldrums

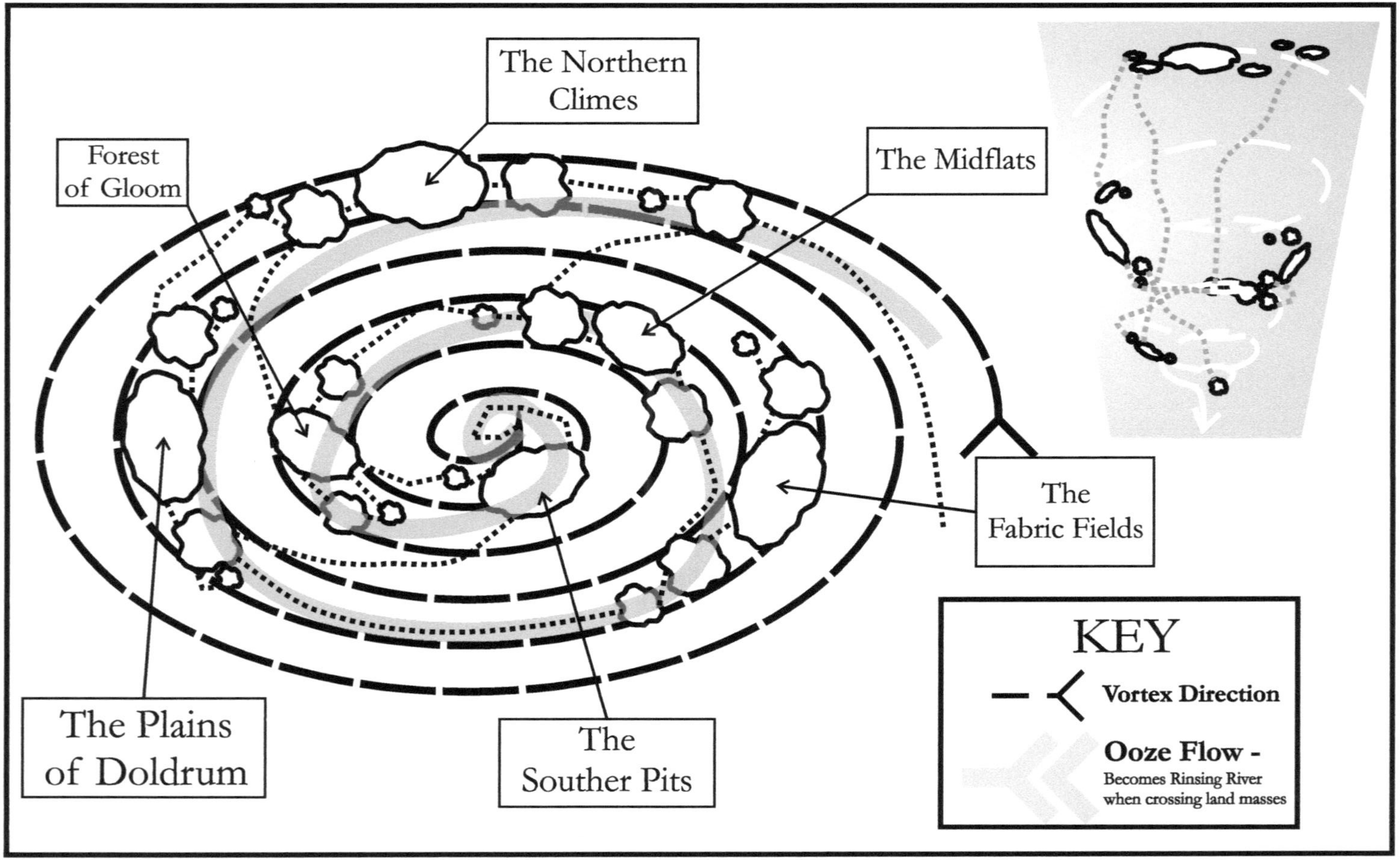

Forest of Gloom

The Plains of Doldrum

The Northern Climes

The Souther Pits

The Midflats

The Fabric Fields

KEY
— Vortex Direction

⟨ Ooze Flow - Becomes Rinsing River when crossing land masses

Region Spotlight: The Midflats

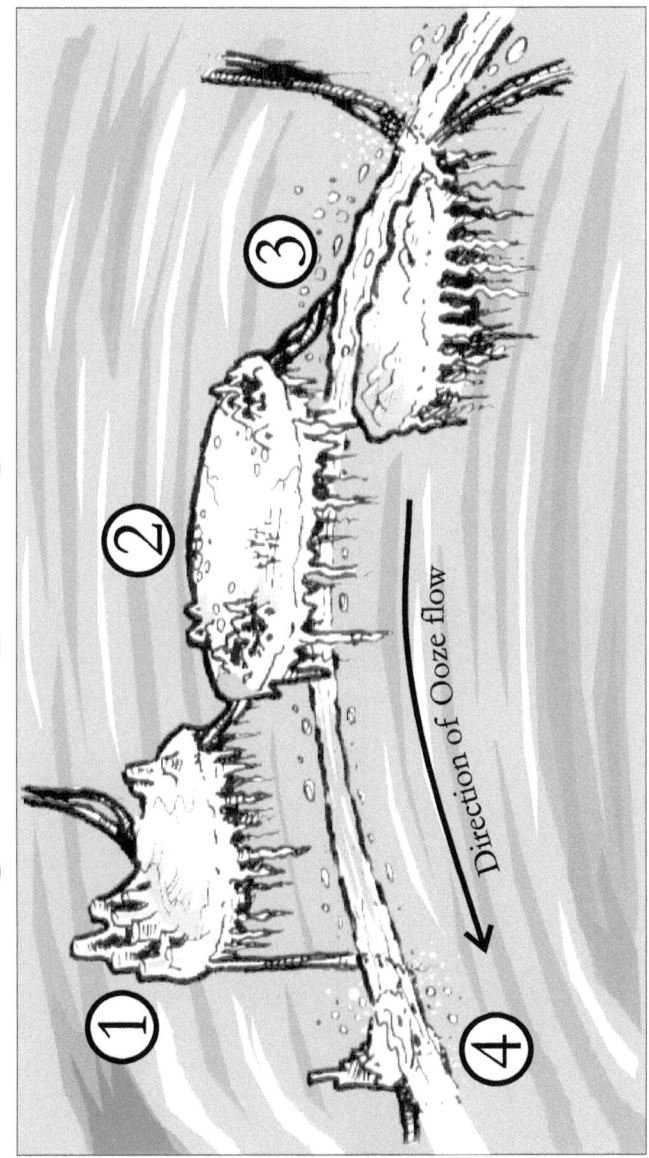

Land masses

1. Blight
Notable features: columnrods
Principal activity: custodians of Blip and the Insole Man Festival

2. Blotch
Notable features: mud blisters
Principal activity: mining mud nutrients

3. Blur
Notable features: rinsing river
Principal activity: healing sleepers

4. Blip, aka. Insole Island
Notable features: stalagrod
Principal activity: hosting the Insole Man Festival

The Midflats are the fourth collection of islands in the Doldrums. The Ooze flows over two of the land masses; Blur, the hilly island that is home to the regions healers; and Blip, also known as Insole Island - the smallest, yet perhaps most important land mass in the Midflats. Blip connects to Dreary, the first island in the region of The Forest of Gloom; Blight connects to Crawl, the first island of The Northern Climes, and Blur attaches to Felt, the second island in The Fabric Fields. For some reason, healers of the rinsing rivers in Midflats appear to produce a higher than average number of muddles - perhaps a curious side-effect of the nutrient rich mud masses that form the Midflats themselves.

Appendix 1: The Garden of Mislaid Garments

#1: The Stocking Eel

The stocking eel is an all too common visitor to The Doldrums; their number has slowly been increasing, with some specimens reported to have grown to huge proportions.

Thought to have originally found its way into the great Rinsing River, the stocking eel is now a common sight in most locations of The Doldrums. Unfortunate stocking eels end up materialising from the human world on dry land, where they quickly wither and die, or are spotted entangled in the lofty branches of The Forest of Gloom.

However, those that end up in the waters of the Doldrums thrive on the nutrients found in the currents, and feed on newly submerged sleepers. Worse still, whole doldrites have been found in the bellies of beached stocking eels, presumably snapped up when the poor victim took an innocent dip in one of the many rivers and lakes that appear on the floating archipelagos that make up their microverse.

Naturally, the origins of the stocking eel begin in the human world, where odd stockings are sucked into the alternate world via the same means used by doldrites on muster missions - namely a water vortex, produced by a washing machine or spin cycle. Although the loss of a single stocking in our world is just as annoying as losing a sock, the stocking has no value to the doldrite, and is considered a predator to them. Because of this, many seekers will freely mutilate any stockings they find while on muster missions, rendering it useless if the stocking under attack were to end up in the Doldrums.

Appendix 2: The Secret World of SOCKMOSIS

The Secret World of SOCKMOSIS -
The trivial, and the not so trivial history of doldrite encounters

Some of the earliest recorded victims of the doldrites were Edwardian dandies - fops who would often be found in the early hours, asleep and inebriated by the fireside. The loosened stockings that hung from their feet were easy prey to primitive doldrites, who would simply slip the stocking from the slack foot. This in turn gave rise to the expression to pull your socks up, as weary servants would soon be in the doldrums when realising that yet another odd stocking had gone missing in the night.

The ugly practice of inserting a branded sock into the mouth of a sleeping human has been recorded several times. The victim will find, upon waking, that a cheap, poorly made sock has been balled up and inserted into the mouth while asleep by an unseen assailant. This event seems to single out snorers, whose dreadful din is despised by doldrites on muster missions. Although now considered highly illegal activity back in the Doldrums, it is thought to still continue in some rare cases, and perhaps forms the origins of the expression putting a sock in it.

One may begin to sympathise with the doldrites when understanding that the human foot has on average a quarter of a million sweat glands, producing up to half a pint of sweat a day. This is almost completely absorbed by socks.

Early experiments indicate that doldrites may be appeased by a simple charm left on socks removed at the end of the day - to invoke the charm, simply whisper 'I'm sorry' into the socks before dropping them in the laundry basket each night.

Dust Bunny Snuff

by Doodlemonkie

1. Dust Bunnies make excellent balls. In fact, they are an essential component in BUNNY BALL.

Appendix 3: The Book of Brutality

Excerpts from the **Book Of Brutality**

The following excerpts were taken from the doldrites Book of Brutality - A huge, ever-expanding litany of abuses committed by humans against members of sock-kind in the human world. Sleepers that are awoken during the process of *cleansing* and *shining* extensively interviewed about their memories, as are those who experience *abuse flashbacks*. The recollections are then committed to this tome, which serves as a continual reminder to the doldrites as to why they are so opposed to the human race.

In this volume, the focus is on uses for sleepers by human owners.

The clutches of the wipers.

Pity the doldrite who is in the paw of a wipers! For they is the vilest of the human peoples. They grip so tight they grip, holdin on an then rubbin an wipin at flat things, again and again, rubbin till the dust is gon. Sometime they spray stinkin chemical onto the flat, an wipe it wiv the clutchd sleeper, wipin the wet chemical on the flat, again and again, until the wet is dry, until the sleeper is wet and the flat is not, but the flat shine now, no more dust, but the sleeper don't shine, he dies a little bit.

Leave the dust alone we say! Let it grow and breed and be the bunneys, and the fluff. But most of all don't make sleepers be wipers. When the Legion comes, we will grip the humans tight in balls and wipe the rinsin river clean wiv their fleshy bodys.

Body Baitin.

This is too horribl to even rite. But ritten it must be. For it is true. Human use sleepers to feed to their beasts. Not for eatin, no, but for baitin. Makin the beast chew down on a twisted and tied sleeper, made into nots, then waved at the beast so as to make it bite an pull an rip f it can. Human like playin wiv beast wiv sleeper, playin a game of tug wiv a poor doldrite, makin it bite hard an not let go until it get tired an bored.

Stupid beast is too stupid to no diffrent. It only dos wat it is tole. Feersom teef an terribl bite is not its fault, it dos wat it is tole by human. So we revenge wiv our plan come Legion day. We feed human to biggest stockin eel we find in Doldrums, we keep it as our beest an trayn it to feed on human. See how he like it!

Makin metal poket.
See those metal circles in some trees at the forest of gloom? The things that fall into Doldrums from human place, the metal circles human love an keep an count. Well human keep these safe, an treasure an covit an even steel them from one another, such is their love of the metal circles.
But sometimes they hide the metal inside a sleeper, makin it so stretched an heavy... it still make into a doldrite when a healer makes him better, but he is never rite. He

loves metal too, cos he was too close to it, havin the circles in his tummy all the time. He comes to life after the rinsin wantin to be near circles for ever an nobody can help that.

Why does the human do this? It matters not. Human loves circles an many other bits an things, so come the Legion we is gonna stuff these bad human wiv all the things they love, until they is heavy an swollen an split apart. So funny to see it will be!

Further Reading

Sockmosis is a series of essays, observations and writings that will give you all you need to know about The Great Sock Horror; a collection of books that, in time, may come to be your survival manual. There are seven books in the series, each tackling a different aspect of sock thievery, as detailed below:

Genesis. Here, we delve into the origins of the species and explore the various theories and hypothesis that shroud the mystery that has been their evolution, focusing on the two main schools of thought; the Big Bump theory and Mother Earth. We also identify the underlying quarrel Doldrites have with humans and the effect their incarceration has on their psyche.

Anatomy of a Doldrite. The diversity of species phenotypes and genotypes are explained, giving advice on correct identification and classification. From there, we explain the fundamentals of civilisation and investigate the internal hierarchy and rites of passage that the doldrites adhere to. Basic health and diseases are also covered in this volume.

Down in the Doldrums. The Doldrums is a world apart from our own, with fascinating landscapes and lifestyles. Both of these subjects are elaborated upon with great concentration particularly afforded to the everyday running of the community. The concept of the state of the doldrums is also discussed; the residual imprint left on our world by their pursuit.

Doldrite Lore. In this volume, the doldrite rituals and customs are explained. Far from being a simple folk, they are governed by ceremonial procedure and customs; however progress has seen a shift in the dynamics within the doldrums as new factions and belief systems develop and are seen to extend to Sapienists and Miserablists. The main factions are discovered and the fundamental practices of each group explained, as well as particularly renowned characters - for example, Quan-Toom Stocking, a brilliant and influential figure, is identified and profiled.

When Worlds Collide. Primarily focusing on the conflict between the hostile doldrites and the human race: here, you will find out all about the doldrites and what they seek in our world; their habits and rituals when they arrive here, and the all-important selection process that forms their raid. You will discover how they commute between their world and ours; how they specially select households - including yours - for their guerrilla missions, and to what extent they will go in order to secure a continuous supply of sleepers.

Survival of the fittest. As When Worlds Collide identifies the technicalities of a successful muster mission, so this volume explains the dangers and the likely problems doldrites will face while on a raid. Diversionary tactics and special training along with the particular hazards associated with portal travel are observed. The many threats that face the doldrites in the human world are catalogued and explored.

Madame Horror's Emporium. The final volume of the series is dedicated to Madame Horrors journal and field notes, gathered over the course of her investigations. Here you will find everything you will need to know to arm yourself against these wicked creatures. There are special sections dedicated to how to lay traps and catch doldrites, the techniques used to probe them for answers and the special process of preserving the horrors for future research.

For more information, or to order any of the above volumes, please visit:

www.sockhorror.com

FORTHCOMING ATTRACTIONS.

FASCINATING NEW PRODUCTS TO HELP WARD OFF THE DOLDRITE PERIL.

We find ourselves in uncertain times, threatened by a hitherto unseen threat. Now, thanks to Madame Horror and her trusty companion, Professor I. Doodlemonkie, we are proud to present a range of articles and applications, each designed with the sole purpose of limiting, perhaps even ending, the acts of tiny terrorism at our toes. Help banish the devilish doldrites back to The Doldrums with these fine wares, and curtail their rambunctious revelries once and for all with one or more purchases from Madame Horror's Emporium.

SOCK HORRORS

Madame Horror is delighted to offer exclusive and unique, one-of-a-kind doldrites from her personal collection of CAPTURED and STUFFED horrors. No two specimens are the same; the colouration, caste and faction of each creature means that EVERY DOLDRITE is truly individual. For photographic representations of the latest victims, please consult the official Sock Horror website.

Bespoke Warding Charms

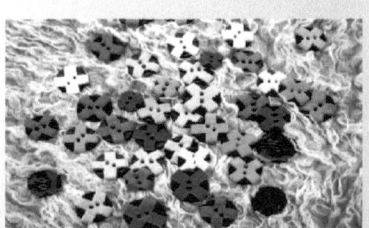

How better to let the doldrites know they are unwelcome than to string up the eyes of unfortunate victims caught by Madame Horror. Rather like a dreamcatcher, these are simply positioned over the bed, or placed in a sock drawer. Similarly, they can be made into items of jewellery for enthusiast collectors.

FORTHCOMING ATTRACTIONS, ONLY ON WWW.SOCKHORROR.COM

The Sock Lovers' Journal

A day to day system for maintaining an inventory of all your family's socks and recording their whereabouts at every stage. Cross reference your sock collection easily by style, colour, day or occasion. Keep a daily journal on the look and feel of your socks and the happiness they bring to the humdrum routine. Also includes techniques to repair wear, notes on the ultimate softeners and preservation practice.

Pewter figurines

Deter those pesky blighters with lifelike Pewter figurines. Collectors' items in their own right, these highly detailed, hand crafted sculptures may also double up as scary totems, warding off any would-be doldrite invaders.

Seekers, muddles, key keepers and more form the range of exclusive miniatures, specially created for SockHorror.com.

New and Exclusive Wares, only from www.sockhorror.com Purveyors of Sock Protection

Catch your Very Own Doldrite!

One of a series of guides dedicated to the capture of doldrites. This booklet contains fundamental information on how to lay a trap (the *Double Dupe*) and includes the instructions on assembly.
The directions enclosed show how to sew an effigy of a doldrite, which then acts as a kind of scarecrow to stand guardian over your <u>Most beloved socks.</u>

Exclusive Art Prints

Immortalised by Professor I Doodlemonkie, these original artworks and prints are representations of the world of The Doldrums and portraits of the creatures that dwell there. Based on extensive research and firsthand experience, these highly desirable pieces comprise a wondrous anthology covering all aspects of <u>The Great Sock Horror.</u>

FORTHCOMING ATTRACTIONS, ONLY ON WWW.SOCKHORROR.COM

ATTENTION SOCKOPHILES!

Keep Your Socks Together!

You never have to worry about the threat of doldrites leaving you with odd socks when you use our *Sock Together* system. Simple and easy to use, this effortless technique will quickly become part of your daily routine, guaranteeing order in your sock drawer. Use these innovative items to pin your socks together throughout the laundry process, keeping your socks secure and paired. This will ensure you always have both socks of a given pair (note that this does not guarantee that the pair will not go missing; you will need the other items in the Sock Horror collection for that).

Make-Your-Own Sock Protectors!

For the true sockophile - a knitting pattern for house-slippers, protecting your socks from unnecessary wear and tear! A labour of love to extend the life of your socks a knitting pattern created for the purpose of providing an extra layer to shield your socks from abrasive surfaces and dirt when in the home, reducing the wear and tear your socks may be subjected to and also decrease the necessity for harsh detergents. Please note that this is a straightforward knitting pattern: however, knowledge of basic knitting techniques is required.

For more information, please consult our website:

www.sockhorror.com

THE SOCK HORROR PLEDGE - Our Promise to you

We, Madame Horror and Doodlemonkie, make this solemn oath to our dear readers and procurers of our finest wares. We hereby pledge to determine the truth of the Great Sock Horror and discover the depths of the dangers we face; to enlighten the world to the dangers of Legion, and to empower the nations to pull their socks up and confront this threat with their best foot forward. Further to this, we promise to enable fellow humans to defend their homes and eradicate all trace of sock madness. Broadly, our aim is to both entertain and enlighten, as well as to change the way you view your laundry... forever.

Sock Horror Socks!

Emblazoned with an icon of a doldrite, these socks are the most *distasteful*, *provocative* and *graven of images* that the offending doldrites could come across. So violent is their reaction to Sock Horror Socks that by purchasing these prime quality socks, you will be guaranteeing yourself an invasion-free household. You will fear no longer of socks stuck in another dimension again.

When asked to describe the effect that Sock Horror Socks have on doldrites, Madame Horror did so in her own inimitable style. 'Imagine a tattoo of your mother, but dead. Now imagine that your mother bears that same tattoo, and it was put there against her wishes. Imagine what it would feel like to see such a thing. Now imagine that this feels about half as bad as a doldrite feels when viewing a Sock Horror Sock.'

So there you have it proof, if any were needed, that Sock Horror Socks may be an essential purchase this year. Winter Bonus: Sock Horror Socks are now 17% more warmer, with seasons greetings from SockHorror.com!

GARTERS

We all know the irritation of lose elastic and the continued droop of a sock or stocking to form unsightly wrinkles round your ankles. Our specialist sock garters are the ideal solution to the problem. Available in numerous designs and colours, we have something for everyone, whether you are an avid sportsman with a real necessity for high performance, or an English gent or Lady of high society, your tastes and requirements will be catered for. Further to function these highly fashionable items have been adopted as the 'in vogue'

accessory for the season and are now presented as neck and wrist adornments. Several styles are available, designed to keep your socks up even in the most extreme of circumstances.

FORTHCOMING ATTRACTIONS, ONLY ON WWW.SOCKHORROR.COM

CAPTURED

Seeker.

The brazen seeker. The most prolific and deadly Sock Horror to venture into our world. Known to be a natural ringleader and the brains behind their raids. Famed for their abilities to locate and steal your socks they are known to be quick thinkers and problem solvers. Cunning and guile are not in short supply when it comes to this mischievous creature.

STUFFED

Muddle.

A mischief maker, the Muddle is as dangerous as any doldrite invading our homes. As 'right hand man' on a muster mission these creatures prey on our unquestioning belief that we are safe in our homes. They seek to cause havoc and deceive and are enduring in their desire to cause us grief.

EXPOSED

Key Keeper.

The orchestrators of our plight. Such creatures are our most dangerous foes as ultimately, control over travel between worlds is governed by these doldrites. Masters of Sockmosis and suckers for heroic missions, they often go against convention and issue keys wherever they believe an assignment will succeed.

OWNED

Herder.

Usually these residents of The Doldrums do not venture out of the safety of their homeland and into our world, but it has been known on occasion that their expertise in fluff is invaluable to the raiding party's success. These normally placid creatures are fearsome when provoked and should be approached with the greatest care.

FORTHCOMING ATTRACTIONS, ONLY ON WWW.SOCKHORROR.COM

As well as visiting the Sock Horror website, readers may also like to know that Madame Horror and Doodlemonkie can be located at the following web portals, where you may find other things of interest:

madamehorror.deviantart.com
doodlemonkie.deviantart.com

www.myspace.com/sockhorror
www.myspace.com/doodlemonkie

www.doodlemonkie.com

Please do stop by and say hello!

www.ingramcontent.com/pod-product-compliance
Ingram Content Group UK Ltd.
Pitfield, Milton Keynes, MK11 3LW, UK
UKHW041228200426
11947UKWH00034B/428